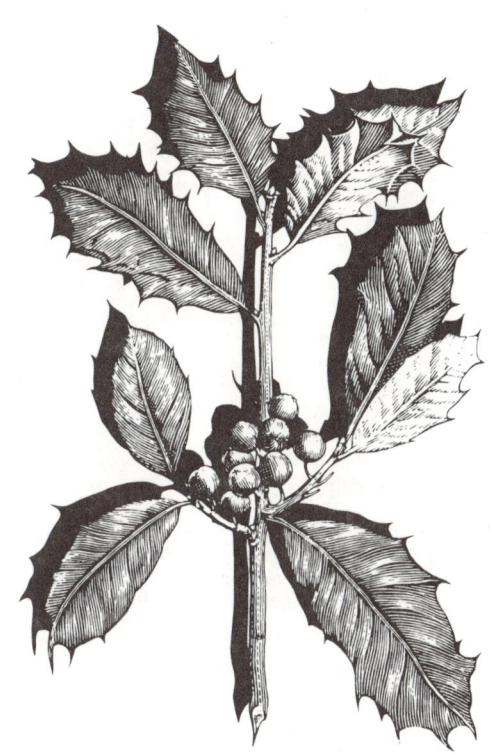

Deck the Halls

A New Service for the Hanging of the Greens

Ralph E. Dessem and Thomas J. Tozer

DECK THE HALLS

Copyright © 1986 by
The C.S.S. Publishing Company, Inc.
Lima, Ohio

You may copy the material in this publication if you are the original purchaser, for use as it was intended (worship material for worship use; educational material for classroom use; dramatic material for staging and production). No additional permission is required from the publisher for such copying by the original purchaser only.

The C.S.S. Publishing Company, Inc., 628 South Main Street, Lima, Ohio 45804.

Second Printing 1986
Third Printing 1987
Fourth Printing 1990

6844 / ISBN 1-89536-827-7   PRINTED IN U.S.A.

A Few Words About This Service

The order of service offered here is intended to be adapted to your own parish, depending upon the design of your sanctuary, the number of participants available, and the technical resources at your disposal, such as microphones, bells, and special lighting.

Sections may be deleted or amended according to whatever best suits your worship needs. Too, the order of service may be arranged differently if you discover ways to add more power and enrichment to its presentation. We do, however, encourage you and your worship planners to give thoughtful consideration before making any substantial changes. The service has been written with careful attention to the sequence of events. Some of it has been created for dramatic effect in order to add visual interest and spiritual impact.

Also, the service was written to allow maximum opportunity for involvement by parishioners of all ages. With the liturgy, Scripture readings, and speaking parts, there is ample room for every adult, young person, and child to take part. Certainly the speaking assignments can be combined or doubled up, depending upon your resources of talent. We urge you, however, to spread around the responsibilities so that as many as possible will be able to share special memories of having been active participants in this celebration.

In order to do justice to this service, we encourage you to prepare for it as you would a full-scale dramatic presentation. Because of the many people involved, with their coordinated entrances, movements, and speaking cues, you will need to block out your action. Careful staging and timing will result in a smoothly flowing, cohesive worship experience. Begin planning and rehearsing well in advance of the worship event. Give your readers/speakers ample opportunity to interpret their words and polish their deliveries. In light of what this sacred season means to all Christians — young and old — you and your worship team should settle for nothing less than the best effort from all participants.

In this service, we have suggested that those who bring forth the greens (Advent wreath, holly and ivy, poinsettias, and Christmas tree) also be the speakers. Although this almost necessitates memorization, we feel that it adds a special informality to the background commentary. Memorization will also add variety and a sense of eye-to-eye communication. The decision, however, is yours. You may, if you wish, divide these assignments and have all your speakers at the front.

Some of the hymn selections are interchangeable, or may be replaced by others that you prefer. There is a specific reason, however, for using the last two music selections. "O Come, All Ye Faithful" invites worshipers to come forward in Christian unity. The postlude (or closing hymn, if you prefer) "Go Tell It On the Mountain" is a directive to share the Good News to the world outside. *Come* forward — *Go* out.

In keeping with the title of this work, you may wish to consider the following as an alternate ending. After the ringing of the bells (steeple bells, chimes, or handbells), and before the benediction, the pastor may invite each worshiper to pick up a piece of holly at the altar. Explain to the gathered congregation that, as they leave the sanctuary during the playing (or singing) of "Deck the Halls" (alternate music), they are to go to different areas of the church and place their holly at appropriate locations for added decoration.

This worship service need not be overly solemn or formal. Instead, it should reflect the exceeding joy of this special season. Let it be a festive occasion for both participants and those in the pews. This is a wonderful opportunity for the pastor and worship planners to involve members of all ages in a memorable worship experience. Make it fun! Make it meaningful!

Tom Tozer
Ralph Dessem

July 1986

Part I.
The Service in Outline

The Order of Service which appears on the following two pages may be photocopied for use in your worship folder. No prior permission from the publisher is required for those who have purchased this resource.

Order of Worship

Setting the Mood

Prelude
The Bells
"Significance of the Bells"
"Significance of the Star"

Procession

Processional Hymn *"Joy To the World"*
Lighting of the Altar Candles
"Significance of the Candles"

The Call to Worship

Leader: Tonight we come together to prepare for the birthday of a King.

People: Tonight we make ready our welcome for God's only Son, Jesus of Nazareth.

Leader: We begin this special and holy season of Advent, the season of *going toward* the birth of Christ.

People: As we renew the special meaning of the Advent season, the season of *going toward* new hope and eternal life,

Leader: Let us clear our minds and open our hearts to the coming of the Lord.

People: Let us also honor his birth by adorning our church for the coming of our King.

Leader: Let our songs and symbols represent our personal rededication to the glory of God and the manifestation of his love through his Son, Jesus Christ.

Together: For God so loved the world that he gave his only begotten Son, that whosoever believeth in him shall not perish but have eternal life.

Hymn *"O Come, O Come, Emmanuel"*

The Prophecy of His Coming

Scripture *Isaiah 9:6-7*
"Significance of the Advent Wreath"
Hymn *"Come, Thou Long Expected Jesus"*
Lighting of the Advent Candle

The Birth of the Christ Child

Scripture *Luke 2:1-7*
Carol *"Away in a Manger"* (children's choir)

Silent Meditation
Pastoral Prayer
"Significance of the Holly and the Ivy"
Hymn *"The Holly and the Ivy"*

Adoration of the Child

Scripture *Luke 2:8-17, Matthew 2:7-11*
Hymn *"Silent Night"*
"Significance of the Poinsettias"

Our Celebration Today

Scripture *John 1:9-14*
"Significance of the Christmas Tree"
Carol *"O Christmas Tree"* (adult choir)
"Significance of Christ In Our Lives Today"
Prayer of Christian Unity
Hymn *"O Come, All Ye Faithful"* (Gathering in the chancel area)

The Bells (Pastor)

Benediction

Postlude

Part II.
The Service in Detail

Setting the Mood

Prelude

(Bells begin chiming, as Prelude ends. Sanctuary lights slowly fade to black. Bells cease.)

Speaker 1: Bells have been used throughout the centuries to call people to worship or to bring them news. Good news and bad news have been heralded by bells. When heirs to royalty were born in European countries, bells would peal. When wars were over, bells would celebrate. Bells ring when Christians die. They ring to call us to God's house. Tonight bells ring to call us to remember the birth which is soon to be celebrated among us: that of the King's heir, our Lord, the Christ.

(A bright star appears above the chancel area.)

Speaker 2: Star of Wonder, star of night,
Star with royal beauty bright,
Westward leading, still proceeding,
Guide us to thy perfect light.

Throughout the ages, astronomers have proposed countless theories about the mysterious light over Bethlehem. Some have calculated it to be the recurrence of Halley's Comet, or the sudden merging of two or more planets. In spite of the theories and speculations, however, and according to ancient manuscripts, a spectacular celestial object *was seen*. Whatever the mysteries surrounding the Bethlehem Star, it has survived the centuries as the symbol of a new birth, a new promise, and a new way of life that has changed the course of human history. It represents the one true "perfect light" that leads us from the darkness of despair to hope eternal. It is the "perfect light" that will not be vanquished.

Procession

(Sanctuary lights come up slowly, as the organ plays the introduction to "Joy to the World." Congregation rises. During the hymn, we have the Procession of choir, acolytes, and readers [if readers are to speak at front]. Following the Processional, the congregation is seated. As the next speaker begins, the acolytes commence lighting the altar candles. *For something really unique, have the acolytes themselves be the speakers, and divide the speaking parts accordingly.)*

Speaker 3: The lighting of candles has been a part of religious worship for centuries. The Hebrews burned candles for eight days as a part of their Feast of Lights. Light has been used by many religious groups to symbolize truth, while darkness has been the universal symbol for evil.

Speaker 4: Since Jesus has been referred to as "the light of the world" in the New Testament, the lighting of candles has become an important part of our Christian worship. Some early Christian leaders stated that the wax of the altar candles represented the body of Christ, while the wick symbolized his soul, and the flame portrayed his divine nature. Candles made from pure beeswax had also served as an emblem of Mary, since this wax comes from virgin bees. This has resulted in the practice of some churches to burn only beeswax candles upon the altar.

Speaker 5: When Joseph and Mary presented Jesus in the temple, Simeon referred to the Christ child as "a light to lighten the Gentiles." From this statement, church leaders have used candles to symbolize the light of Christ shining throughout a sin-darkened world.

Speaker 6: As we light these candles upon the altar, we symbolize his coming into the world of sin and evil, war and strife, stress and turmoil, suffering and death. He came to bring hope and help to those who were held captive by oppression, and to guide them to personal peace and joy through the illumination of his message of the love of God.

The Call to Worship

Leader: Tonight we come together to prepare for the birthday of a King.

People: Tonight we make ready our welcome for God's only Son, Jesus of Nazareth.

Leader: We begin this special and holy season of Advent, the season of *going toward* the birth of Christ.

People: As we renew the special meaning of the Advent season, the season of *going toward* new hope and eternal life,

Leader: Let us clear our minds and open our hearts to the coming of the Lord.

People: Let us also honor his birth by adorning our church for the coming of our King.

Leader: Let our songs and symbols represent our personal rededication to the glory of God and the manifestation of his love through his Son, Jesus Christ.

Together: For God so loved the world that he gave his only begotten Son, that whosoever believeth in him shall not perish but have eternal life.

Invocation: Our Father in heaven, in the weeks to come, our attention to this blessed and holy event, the birth of your Son, will be continually distracted. Help us to distinguish between the secular and the sacred, and to remember the true meaning of our joy and excitement. Help us to refocus our minds and hearts on your loving and most precious gift to us, your Son, our Lord and Savior, Jesus Christ. Amen

Hymn "O Come, O Come, Emmanuel"

The Prophecy of His Coming

Scripture Isaiah 9:6-7

(The four speakers may also be the ones who bring the Advent wreath down the center aisle and place it at the front. Or if the Advent wreath is already in place, the speakers may appear from the sides of the chancel area and cross to the front.)

Speaker 7: Advent is a time of expectation, and this is

symbolized not only by the four-week period of preparation, but also by the lighting of an Advent candle on each Sunday of the season. The flame of each new candle reminds the worshiper that something is happening, but something more is still to come. The Advent season will not be complete until all four candles are lighted, with the central Christ candle also burning brightly on Christmas Eve or Christmas Day.

Speaker 8: The tradition of the Advent wreath is traced back to an old Scandinavian custom that celebrated the coming of light after a season of darkness. In that day, candles were placed on the edge of a horizontal wheel. As the wheel was spun around, the lighted candles would blend into a continuous circle of light. Today we use a circle of evergreen to remind us of the continuous power of God, which knows no beginning nor ending.

Speaker 9: There is also symbolizm in the colors of the candles in the Advent wreath. The three purple, or white, candles symbolize the coming of Christ from the royal line of David. He is coming as the King of Kings as well as the Prince of Peace. The pink candle is lighted on the third Sunday of the Advent season. This candle symbolizes joy; its use goes back to the Latin church which asked the worshipers to fast during this period of time.

Speaker 10: A progression is noted in the lighting of the candles of the Advent wreath, beginning with the first, symbolizing *expectation*. The second reminds us that we are involved in a season of *preparation* for the celebration of the coming of Christ. *Proclamation* is the theme of the third candle, as we proclaim that Christ brought joy to the world when he appeared. The *revelation* of God's love for all humankind is portrayed by the lighting of the fourth candle. The culmination of the season comes on Christmas Eve, or Christmas Day, as the Christ candle is lighted. We join in rejoicing over the fact that the promise of long ago has now been fulfilled.

Hymn "Come, Thou Long Expected Jesus"

Lighting of the Advent Candle (may take place during the singing)

The Birth of the Christ Child

Scripture Luke 2:1-7

Carol "Away in a Manger" (children's choir)

Silent Meditation

Pastoral Prayer

(Speakers place holly and ivy throughout sanctuary as they speak.)

Speaker 11: Have you ever wondered why we talk about the "hanging of the greens"? Or why an *evergreen* is called an *evergreen*? And why *Christmas greens* are traditionally used to emphasize the nativity? Green represents renewal, new life, freshness, and rebirth. Plants such as pine, fir, holly, ivy, and mistletoe are called *evergreens* because they do not die; through the seasons of the year, they remain *ever-green. Ever-alive.* It is no wonder then that we deck our sanctuary and halls with evergreens during this Advent season. Advent is the season of preparation for the coming of the Christ, God's gift to us of new and eternal life.

Speaker 12: The many legends of the holly include a dark side as well as a brighter side. It has been said that what was once called the "holy tree" somehow became *holly* through a corruption of the English language. Even before the dawn of Christianity, the eternal green leaves of the holly tree gave it an aura of mystery and reverence.

Speaker 13: Primitive tribes believed that hanging holly in their shelters would bring them good fortune. They also believed its mysterious powers would chase away witches and evil spirits.

Speaker 14: Early Christians wore holly as they entered the church, convinced this would give them supernatural powers. It was their belief that the burning bush through which God spoke to Moses was the holly — or holy — tree. Many believed that Christ's crown of thorns was fashioned from holly leaves. And that after the crown was pressed down on his head, his blood turned the white berries to the red berries we recognize today.

Speaker 15: Holly was so revered for its ability to defy death, it is said that wherever Jesus walked on earth, holly sprang up in his footsteps.

Speaker 16: Ivy, too, is rich in symbolism. In the Middle Ages, ivy was used extensively for Christmas decorating. It was considered a symbol of love because of its clinging habit of growth. Holly and ivy are often associated together in legends because of the holly's sturdiness and the ivy's tenaciousness. Both have the incredible ability to survive and to grow.

Speaker 17: We decorate our sanctuary with holly and ivy because of their link through the ages with beauty, endurance, and permanence. And though they are steeped in legend and superstition, their quality of life over death is fitting and proper for the birth of the one who offers each of us life *beyond* death.

Hymn "The Holly and the Ivy"

THE HOLLY AND THE IVY

> The holly and the ivy,
> When they are both full grown,
> Of all the trees that are in the wood,
> The holly bears the crown.

Refrain: *The rising of the sun*
And the running of the deer,
The playing of the merry organ,
Sweet singing of the choir.

> The holly bears a blossom,
> As white as the lily flower,
> And Mary bore sweet Jesus Christ,
> To be our sweet Saviour.

Refrain

> The holly bears a berry,
> As red as any blood,
> And Mary bore sweet Jesus Christ,
> To do poor sinners good.

Refrain

The holly bears a prickle,
As sharp as any thorn,
And Mary bore sweet Jesus Christ,
On Christmas day in the morn.

Refrain

The holly bears a bark,
As bitter as any gall,
And Mary bore sweet Jesus Christ,
For to redeem us all.

Refrain

(Music can be found in *The Oxford Book of Carols*, by Percy Dearmer, R. Vaughn, and Martin Shaw.)

Adoration of the Child

Scripture **Luke 2:8-17, Matthew 2:7-11**

Hymn **"Silent Night"**

(The poinsettias should be brought into the sanctuary from various locations and placed accordingly. Those who bring them in may also be the speakers for the following, unless otherwise desired.)

Speaker 18: The most popular flower of the Advent-Christmas season is the bright red poinsettia. Actually, the red petals are not the blossoms; they are the small yellow clusters found at the center. Somehow the red and green leaves of the plant give to Christmas an added touch that would not be the same without them.

Speaker 19: This attractive flower was discovered growing wild in Mexico by Dr. Joel Roberts Poinsett who served as our first foreign minister to that country from 1825 to 1829. In Mexico the plant was referred to as the Flower of the Holy Night or the Flame Leaf. Dr. Poinsett brought several of the new plants to America where a Philadelphia nurseryman developed it into the type of flower we see today.

Speaker 20: Many legends have grown up around the poinsettia. One is that it was merely a weed that grew in Mexico, until it was placed at the feet of the Virgin Mary by a poor peasant girl who had no other gift to bring. As it touched the feet of the statue, it was transformed immediately into a flower of scarlet brilliance.

Another legend states that blood fell from the broken heart of a young Mexican girl, and a poinsettia grew where each drop fell.

Speaker 21: This beautiful flower speaks to us symbolically in several ways. First of all, the star-shaped formation of red leaves calls to mind the star which shone at that first Christmas. In a less joyous sense, the color of the flower is blood red. This reminds us of the blood of the male infants killed by Roman soldiers as King Herod sought to eliminate any threat to his throne. We sometimes forget this part of the story which made the trip of Mary, Joseph, and the Christ child to Egypt a necessity. The color of the flower also symbolizes the fact that the *Babe* of Bethlehem's manger became the *Savior* of the world, as he shed his blood upon the cross of Calvary.

Our Celebration Today

Scripture John 1:9-14

(We suggest that the speakers also be the ones who carry the Christmas tree down the aisle and place it at the front wherever desired. Speakers 22 and 23 should deliver their lines as the tree is brought forth. Speakers 24 and 25 should deliver their lines as the tree is being decorated. Other young people may help decorate the tree. If need be, the decorating can continue during the singing of "O Christmas Tree" by the adult choir.)

Speaker 22: The evergreen tree has been a symbol for Christmas and the center of holiday festivities for many years. The green color of the tree symbolizes growth; it also represents everlasting life in the midst of winter.

It is hard to tell just when the use of a tree at the Christmas season began. However, it was probably first used in Scandinavia. Records tell of its use there in the eighth century, when St. Boniface persuaded the Druids to replace the oak tree of their pagan ceremonies with a fir tree that symbolized eternal life.

Speaker 23: The most famous story about the early use of the evergreen tree at Christmas centers around Martin Luther. As he walked through the forest one starry night, with snow covering the ground, he marveled at the beauty of the starlight as it shone upon the branches of the fir trees. When he tried to tell his family of the glory and beauty of the forest, they failed to comprehend what he had seen. He then brought a pine tree into the house and placed candles upon it to represent the twinkling of the stars.

Speaker 24: The earliest use of the Christmas tree in America is also not known. However, a German tailor, August Imgard, set up a fir tree in his home at Wooster, Ohio, in 1847, and decorated it. The first tree to appear in a church was in Cleveland, Ohio, in 1851. Some members of the congregation thought the act was sacrilegious, and were very critical of their pastor. Few trees appeared in churches in the mid-nineteenth century, since many still considered it to be a pagan custom. However, the tree has now become a symbol of the glory of God and his promise of eternal life.

Speaker 25: Many of the decorations we place on the Christmas tree symbolize various aspects of our Christian faith. An ancient legend tells of a poor woman who could only provide a small, sparsely-decorated tree for her children. One night, however, spiders spun webs throughout the tree as a reward for the woman's goodness; and the Christ child turned the webs into silver and gold. Thus, the tinsel which we place on the tree represents the miraculous power of the Christ to bring us hope in the midst of our despair. The large star at the top of the tree reminds us of the adoration of the Christ child by the wise men. An angel in place of the star calls our attention to the majesty of God and his heavenly throng. In additon to those, our tree also bears the following Christian symbols: (Speaker should point out the various symbols and their meaning. This is optional, depending upon the extent of your tree decorating.).

(If the decorating carries over into the singing of the carol, the tree may be lighted at that time.)

Carol "O Christmas Tree" (adult choir)

Speaker 26: There is a danger in coming together year after year to celebrate the birth of a child that occurred nearly 2,000 years ago. We regard the coming of Christ as a significant historical event; thus, we tend to view it in the context of an ancient era. It is an event that we *observe*. And, as observers, we place ourselves outside of it, looking on, celebrating the birth of a baby long ago rather than the rebirth of our lives today. It is God within each of us that makes this Advent season a time of renewed hope and a celebration of new life. Let us rejoice together in the birth of our Savior, Jesus Christ, those many centuries ago. But let us also bring his birth into the context of our lives today, at this very moment.

Speaker 27: Martin Luther once said: "There are some of us ... who think to ourselves, "If I had only been there! How quick I would have been to help the Baby. I would have washed his linen. How happy I would have been to go with the shepherds to see the Lord lying in the manger!' Yes, we would. We say that because we know how great Christ is. But if we had been there at that time, we would have done no better than the people of Bethlehem. Why don't we do it now? We have Christ in our neighbor."

Speaker 28: So let us stand right now and join hands with our neighbors in an unbroken chain of Christian love and unity.

(Pause until worshipers have done so.)

Advent is the *going toward* greater love among people. Advent is the *going toward* greater peace and harmony among people. Advent is the *going toward,* as the carol says, "the dawn of God's redeeming grace." This is an Advent for each of us. We stand at the threshold of decision. We can be faithful observers of a birthday that occured nearly 2,000 years ago — or we can be loving servants to the Christ who walks among us today.

Prayer of Christian Unity (Pastor)

Hymn "O Come, All Ye Faithful"

(At this point, the congregation is invited to proceed as near as possible to the chancel area during the singing. If several verses are sung, they may wish to carry their hymnals. Hymnals can be left on the front pews as worshipers leave the sanctuary.)

(Following the hymn, bells ring several times, then cease.)

Pastor: (after the ringing of the bells) **There is a legend of a great cathedral whose bells suddenly refused to ring. Nobody knew why. Finally, a messenger announced that God had decided not to let the bells ring until the gifts of his people were once more satisfactory. On Christmas Eve, therefore, the people brought the most expensive gifts they had. But the bells did not ring. The king came and laid his crown at the altar. But the bells did not ring. Toward the end of the service, a small lad, a beggar's son, went forward and put his one and only coin on the altar — a coin he had intended to use to buy a loaf of bread for his family. Then he knelt to pray. Suddenly, the beautiful bells pealed forth as never before.**
  (The bells resume ringing immediately and continue through the benediction.) **May the bells we hear this season call to our remembrance that great gift which changed the history of the world, the gift to us of God's own Son.**

Benediction

Postlude

(The postlude may instead be a closing hymn sung by the congregation, if so desired. Either "Deck the Halls" or "Go Tell It On the Mountain" can be found in most hymnals. If the closing hymn option is used, worshipers can remain down front with their hymnals and join together in song.)